Wicca

Thorsons First Directions

Wicca

Vivianne Crowley

Thorsons
An Imprint of HarperCollinsPublishers
77–85 Fulham Palace Road,
Hammersmith, London W6 8JB

The Thorsons website address is:
www.thorsons.com

Published by Thorsons 2000

10 9 8 7 6 5 4 3 2 1

Text derived from *Principles of Wicca*, published by Thorsons, 1997

Editor: Nicky Vimpany
Design: Wheelhouse Creative Ltd.
Photography by Henry Allen and PhotoDisc Europe Ltd.

A catalogue record for this book
is available from the British Library

ISBN 0007103352

Printed and bound in Hong Kong

Contents

Wicca

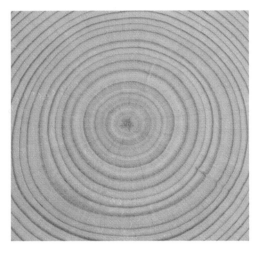

is the ancient art, craft and

religion of Witchcraft

Wicca is...

Witchcraft is not merely a system of magic. Wicca is a Pagan mystery religion of Goddess and God. It is also a Nature religion.

The Witch is a magic-maker and worships a Goddess – the Great Mother Goddess – and the Horned God. In Greek mythology he is Pan and, to the Celts, Herne or Cernunnos. Wicca is based on remnants of simple Pagan traditions handed down in folklore and country custom. Onto these have been grafted more sophisticated beliefs from the more formal Paganisms of Rome, Greece and Egypt, and from the initiatory mystery traditions. Wicca involves the development of magical psychic powers, but hand in hand with the wisdom to use them. An initiatory system of spiritual development is an intrinsic part of the tradition.

For women, Wicca is a spiritual path in which we can worship the Divine in its female form – as Goddess. Many women come to Wicca from feminism. They have re-evaluated the word 'Witch' and realized that it involves the use of the innate powers of the Wise Woman. However, it is not only women who seek the Goddess. Men too are attracted by Wicca's vision of deity as both Goddess and God. Despite the popular image, both men and women can be Witches. The traditional male Witch is a countryman. He is one who is in touch with the elements, who has worked the land, healed a bird's broken wing or the illness of a child; one who loves the Goddess and knows both Goddess and God.

The growing environmental awareness in society today makes Wicca more and more attractive. Wicca honours the Divine as manifest in Nature. The Earth is our spiritual mother and we sense that the Divine is not 'out there' but all around us. Nature itself is sacred and holy, a manifestation of the Divine Life Force. Greenpeace, environmental action, vegetarianism and animal rights are all manifestations of a reawakening spirit of reverence towards the Earth. This was natural and instinctive to our ancestors, but recent centuries of urban living have suppressed it.

Initiation, in the sense of a personal transformatory experience of the Divine, is undoubtedly an attraction of Wicca for some. Some Wiccan traditions have three or more initiation ceremonies that mark transitions through spiritual change. Such rites can be powerful spiritual and psychological events which are life-enhancing and life-changing.

Origins of Wicca

Wicca's history is that of natural magic, the Pagan mystery traditions, such as those of Egypt and Eleusis, and of Celtic spirituality. Wicca draws on mysticism, astrology, runes, tarot and, in modern times, on insights from psychology. It also draws on the traditions of healing of body and of soul.

Although the practice I describe here is European in origin, Wicca represents universal beliefs. Similar traditions exist all over the world; wherever indigenous spirituality has not been suppressed.

The Wiccan revival in the twentieth century began in England, sacred Albion, home of Glastonbury, Stonehenge and the legends of the Grail. This is perhaps no accident. The idea that the Western islands of Europe were Holy Ground and sacred soil is a long-held tradition. The greatest Druid training schools in the Celtic era were in Britain and Ireland and in Medieval times, scholars claimed that Britain was given to their ancestors by the Goddess Diana.

These Pagan links are part of the reason why Witchcraft has revived more quickly in England than in other parts of Europe. Another is England's remoteness from Rome. This meant that it was Christianized later than some parts of Europe and with the Protestant Reformation could more easily break from Rome. English Protestantism was not a fanatical variety. It did not engage in Witch persecutions with the same enthusiasm as some of its Catholic and Protestant neighbours. People often think of Europe as having been Christian for 2,000 years, but this is not the case. Paganism and Christianity were still struggling over a thousand years after this time.

On the fringes of Western Europe many Pagan ideas endured in ways they could not have done elsewhere. Witchcraft and Paganism survived in rural areas as part of the folk traditions and folk medicine of the people. This does not mean that the ruling classes of society were not exposed to these folk traditions. Communal festivities such as May Day were celebrated by all.

Despite this, Witchcraft would have remained an underground tradition if it was not for the work of one man, Gerald Gardner, who became familiar through his radio broadcasts, books and media publicity. He was one of the first Witches in the twentieth century to talk publicly about his beliefs and to share them with others. Gerald Gardner's two most well known books *Witchcraft Today* (1954) and *The Meaning of Witchcraft* (1959) produced a huge surge of interest, inspiring a movement that has spread around the world.

Why Wicca?

People come to Wicca for many reasons. Some seek occult power and knowledge. Some are drawn to Wicca by feminism and the role of the Goddess; others by ecological awareness and reverence for Nature; still others seek spiritual transformation. Magic is an attraction for some. Gerald Gardner, one of the 'founding fathers' or revivers of modern Wicca once wrote:

'Witchcraft was, and is, not a cult for everybody. Unless you have an attraction to the occult, a sense of wonder, a feeling that you can slip for a few minutes out of the world into the world of faery, it is of no use to you.'

Practising Wicca

Before you delve any further into Wicca, try out some of the exercises in this book and see how well they work for you. If you find that these simple introductions to the world of Wicca enhance your life, then you may want to explore Witchcraft further. If so, how do you go about it? There are many different ways, but there are four basic paths you can pursue.

There are two solitary paths

- One is that of the traditional Witch, otherwise known as the Wise Woman, Cunning Man or Hedgewitch.
  Hedgewitchery is less about ritual and more about the Craft of the Witch. If you want to follow this path, a good starting point is Rae Beth's beautiful book *Hedgewitch*. Another useful book is Marian Green's A *Witch Alone*. A skill you will need on this path is the traditional one of herbalism. There are many good books on herbalism and training is available through reputable schools.

You will need to know a lot about traditional country weather lore, and an enthusiasm for gardening will be a help.

- Another solitary path is that of more modern teach-yourself Witchcraft, which you develop yourself with the aid of books and maybe attending occasional workshops or gatherings.

   British Witch Doreen Valiente, who died in 1999, was one of the first advocates of the approach that you did not need to join a coven to be a Witch but could train yourself. She wrote many helpful books, including *Witchcraft for Tomorrow*, which bridge the gap between traditional Craft and modern approaches. American male Witch Scott Cunningham, who died a few years ago, was a modern advocate of this approach. His books, which include *Living Wicca: A Further Guide for the Solitary Practitioner*, are widely available.

There are also two sorts of coven Witchcraft.

- One is the modern do-it-yourself variety, which has flourished in the United States, often influenced by the feminist movement.

   If you have a group of friends who want to create a coven, but do not want to join one of the initiatory traditions, the American Witch Starhawk's famous book *The Spiral Dance* describes coven practice in a modern, eclectic, feminist-oriented coven. Doreen Valiente's books are also useful for those forming groups.

- Another type of coven Witchcraft is more structured and is often known today as Traditional Initiatory Witchcraft or sometimes Traditional British Witchcraft. This involves joining a coven that is part of an initiatory tradition.

  This is the best route for those who prefer a more structured approach and want to learn from people more experienced than themselves. For more information about this type of Witchcraft, I suggest you read my book *Wicca: The Old Religion in the New Millennium*. Some traditional initiatory groups call themselves simply 'Traditional'. Others follow traditions derived from particular covens. North America has many traditional and non-traditional groups: a comprehensive listing of over 200 of these is available in Margot Adler's invaluable book *Drawing Down the Moon*.

Groups and solo

Even if we want to join a group, it is good to practise our ritual work alone sometimes. It is also good to interact with others. There is a very special magic in working with a group of people and seeing something emerge that is much greater than the sum of the parts. The solitary path can be just that – solitary. It is helpful to be able to share our inner hopes and aspirations with others of like mind. This may not necessarily involve joining a group. In most countries where Wicca is well-developed, there are opportunities to attend the occasional social gathering or workshop.

Initiatory traditions

We do not need to be initiated or to join a group or be trained by others to be a Witch. We can make our own spells and rituals and, if our magical ability and spiritual intent are good, they will work. However, an important principle in Witchcraft and magic is that 'old is good'. Spells that have been used time upon time and rituals that have been repeated regularly build up an energy of their own. If a rite is repeated by different people all over the world, it becomes easier and easier.

Most Wiccan traditions have three levels of initiation. Before the first degree, some covens also have a neophyte initiation. This involves a period of dedication and training. The would-be Witch may be able to attend sabbats with the coven and get to know them, so that both coven and trainee can see if they are mutually suited.

The Elements

The Wiccan universe is a holistic universe.
All of creation is alive. People, animals,
plants, trees, rocks, crystals, molecules,
even atoms, have their own purposes and
spiritual force. In our holistic universe, it is
not only the animal, plant and mineral life
of our planet that is alive. It is the planet
itself. Distinguished scientist James
Lovelock developed this idea in his *Gaia
Hypothesis*. Together, plants, animals and
minerals interact in such a way as to seem
part of a living being, a greater whole. This
is the biosphere, or Gaia.

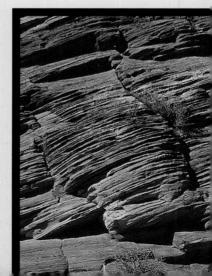

Within our interacting, holistic universe, there are many different types of energy and there are many ways of categorizing them. All spiritual traditions have different ways of looking at the universe. In a sense all these systems and categories are artificial. However, in the magical universe an ancient Greek idea still works well. This is the idea that the material universe consists of energy in four basic states – Earth, Air, Fire and Water. Beyond material creation is a fifth state – Ether or Spirit.

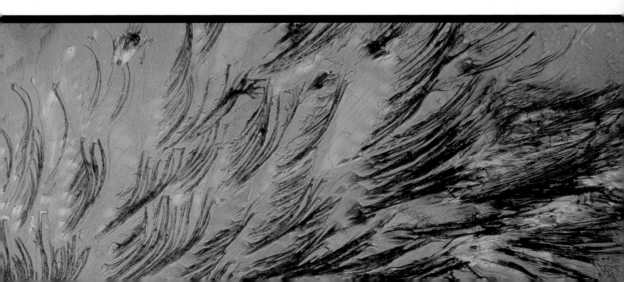

Air

Air is the realm of mind, the brain, the intellect and logical linear thought. The Airy side of us is the part that wants to learn, which is curious and tries to understand the true nature of things. It is youthful, light and energetic. Air can be quickness of thought, lightness of being, humour, the joy of life. Air values the new and untried, and wants to learn new things whatever the price. Air signs are good at starting anew, and throwing old things away. Air divides things into categories. It separates one thing from another. It gets to the point and is not 'woolly-minded'. Working with the Air element can help to develop objectivity. Sometimes impersonal and detached, Air is the sign of the law and can be hard-nosed in its approach.

The zodiac signs ruled by Air: **Aquarius**, **Libra** and **Gemini**.

Fire

Fire warms the blood and governs sexuality. Fire is activity, making things happen, excitement, entertainment, liveliness, the swiftness of the arrow. Fire is important if we are to act in the world. It is renewing and purifying. Fire transforms, changes, destroys, but clears the ground for new growth. It is also associated with a hot temper and war-like aspect. Fire can provoke arguments, but also brings us energy, new life and vigour.

Fire is flamboyant and colourful. Fire's passion can foster love of life and creativity. Fire is freedom and passion: the energy and the warmth of love as well as the desire to consume. Risk-taking is another aspect of Fire – courage or recklessness depending on how one views it. Fire is impatient. Once it gets going it does not stop until it has burned itself out. We often relate intuition to fire.

The zodiac signs ruled by Fire:
Aries, **Leo** and **Sagittarius**.

Earth

This is the element of the physical body, our flesh and bones. Earth has the qualities of steadfastness, dependability, endurance, protection. It is realistic and 'down to earth'. However, it also has a more pleasurable side. It is sex and sensuality, sometimes to excess. Earth can also be greedy about food and money. Earth is important in Pagan initiatory rites. Stone Age cave paintings had magical purposes. They were reached only by dark, difficult journeys through caverns. Here young people were told the myths of their tribe: stories that linked the tribe to its Gods and explained the mysteries of life and death.

   There can be a great sense of peace in Earth meditations, but it is important to remember Earth's destructive potential. However, Earth is patient. She can endure and rectify our mistakes – given time.

The zodiac signs ruled by Earth: **Taurus, Virgo** and **Capricorn**.

Exercise:
Experiencing the elements

1 Wicca is an Earth-based religion, so it is important for you to tune in to the natural world and the seasonal cycle. Spend two days doing as much as you can to experience the physical presence of all four elements. Get outside. Walk upon, touch, dig, smell, feel the Earth. Feel the Sun and wind on your skin. Paddle in a stream or walk in the rain.

2 Note the quality of the Earth on which you walk, the Air you breathe, the Water you drink or which falls on you as rain, the Sun that warms you. Meditate on what these elements might be saying to you.

3 To feel the Earth and its energy, try placing your hand on the ground and feeling its pulse. If you are stuck in the inner city, go to a city park. If this is impossible, walk the streets and try to connect with the Earth beneath the layers of concrete. If you are not able to go out, use a bowl of earth or perhaps a stone. Hold it and feel its qualities while you meditate on it.

4 Do the same with the other elements. Water is seas and rivers and pools and rain. Again, if you cannot get out, meditate with a bowl of water.

5 Air is, of course, the wind. Feel it against you, both physically and through meditation.

6 For Fire, light a fire, either outside or in your hearth. Remember that Fire is also the Sun and you can meditate on Fire by burning a candle.

7 Keep a symbol of each element in your home: a bowl of earth and one of water; a candle for Fire; for Air, something light like a bird's feather or something that makes sounds such as wind chimes.

8 Spend a day meditating on each of these elements. Which elements do you feel you have in abundance in your personality? Which do you need to develop and why? Record all your thoughts and insights on the elements. 'Earth' yourself after each meditation by eating and drinking something.

Exercise:

The elements in your life

1 A Wiccan altar usually has symbols of all four elements on it, but there may be times in your life when you need to encourage the energy of one particular element into your life.

2 One way of doing this is to make an altar for the element that is lacking in your life. If you lack energy and are timid and unconfident, make a Fire altar. Use a red altar cloth, red flowers, a red-leafed potted plant, berries, red candles. To represent Earth, find a piece of red sandstone or other red rock. Use a bowl of red glass for your Water. For Air, burn incense that seems hot and fiery. Place some tarot cards from the suite of wands on the altar if you have them.

3 Having set up your altar, light the candles and incense. Sit in front of the altar and meditate on how and where you can bring Fire into your life. Ask the powers of Fire to help you use them wisely and well in their appropriate place, but not in excess. Spend some time every day for a week meditating upon Fire.

4 In the second week, take the Fire energy into your everyday life. Put something from your Fire altar such as your red rock or plant in your workplace. Wear something red when you need to display your Fire energy. Take to using a red pen! All these are simple things but they are working on the age-old magical principle of sympathetic magic.

5 Similarly, if you need to display more love and sympathy, make a Water altar. If you need to sharpen your thinking use Air. To bring stability, inner strength and peace into your life, work with the element of Earth.

Nature

Attuning ourselves to the seasonal cycle is one of the most important things about becoming a Witch. This may seem surprising, but Wicca is a nature religion. The Divine is in-dwelling in Nature and Nature is its cloak and garment. By celebrating the seasonal festivals we reconnect with the rhythms of Nature and we reconnect with the Divine.

The festivals

Wicca has eight major festivals. These start at Sunset and last until Sunset the next day. Four are solar festivals, whose timing is determined by the relationship of the Sun to the Earth. These are:

- **Winter Solstice** or **Yule** (the shortest day), around 21/22 December
- **Summer Solstice** or **Midsummer** (the longest day), around 21/22 June
- The **Spring** and **Autumn Equinoxes** when the hours of darkness and light are equal. Around the 20/21 March and 21/22 September

In the southern hemisphere, in Australia for instance, the seasons are reversed. The Winter Solstice is on June 21.

The four other Wiccan festivals are Celtic in origin. These are:

- **Imbolc**, or **Candlemas**, February 1/2
- **Beltane** or **May Eve** on April 30/May 1
- **Lughnasadh**, also known as **Lammas** or **Loaf Mass**, July 31/August 1
- **Samhain** (pronounced sow-in) also known as **All Hallow's Eve**, October 31/November 1.

Ideally Witches celebrate their festivals on the correct date, but if the correct day is impractical we can have our celebration at another time, as near the date as possible.

Imbolc

In the temperate parts of the northern hemisphere, Imbolc or
Candlemas brings the awakening of the life force when the first green
shoots of bulbs appear. This is a hopeful time. Life is stirring again.
The days grow noticeably longer. Traditional English Witches still call
this festival by its name in the Christian calendar – Candlemas, the
feast of candles. Both Pagan and Christian festivals are sacred to the
Virgin Goddess whose image was absorbed into that of Mary.

   Magically, Imbolc is a good time to plan new enterprises and to make
the first moves towards bringing them into actuality. Candle magic and
magic for new beginnings are traditional at this time. However, it is
best to proceed cautiously. It is time to design and plan, to dig
foundations rather than to build.

Spring Equinox

Spring Equinox is the turning of the year, when light overcomes darkness. Lengthening days bring new growth. The sap rises. The sexual urge awakens in the animal world and our own.

Spring Equinox celebrates the fertility of the land. It is a time to sow seeds both literally and symbolically. Often seeds imbued with magical intents are sown at Spring Equinox. On a psychological level, the nurturing of seedlings is a constant reminder of the magical wish that was made with their planting.

The urge of Spring is to do, create, change, to get rid of the old and bring in the new. This is a valuable energy and we need it in our lives, but we also need to treat it with balance and common sense.

Beltane

Beltane means 'bright fire' in Gaelic. In Ireland, bonfires were lit and cattle driven through them to rid their hides of parasites. To leap the bonfire was to take the flame inside yourself. The flame would bring new life; so even today Wiccan couples who want to conceive will leap the Beltane fire. Traditionally, Beltane was a time for fertility magic. May Day ceremonies included men and women dancing together around phallic may-poles with women garlanded in flowers and strong ale flowing.

In European tradition, the God appears at May Day in the guise of Jack-in-the-Green or the Green Man. In English country customs, the Green Man was disguised by his garment of leaves and in the freedom of anonymity could do what he willed. This might also have solved some couples' fertility problems.

Summer Solstice

Summer Solstice, the Longest Day, is the season of oak leaves and roses, symbols of God and of Goddess. Although both God and Goddess are present at Beltane and Midsummer, Beltane seems much more a Goddess festival; whereas Midsummer celebrates the God.

Midsummer rites are often dedicated to the crowning of the solar king and the dedication of his male energy to the service of the Goddess, her people and her land. Paradoxically, this time is both the height of the Sun and the beginning of its decline. After the peak there is nowhere to go but down.

Midsummer is a good time for men to do magic to help them in their everyday lives and for both sexes to do magic to help them with worldly matters – careers, houses, money. These are all the worldly but essential things we need for our material existence.

Lughnasadh

Lughnasadh is the Irish word for the August Eve festival. The alternative name, Lammas, is a Saxon word which means Loaf Mass. At Loaf Mass, the first bread was baked with the new wheat of the year. Try picking an ear of wheat. Hold it and meditate upon it. The ripened wheat has not the smoothness of youth, but the ripeness of age. It is dry, but new life can spring from it. One message of Lammas is about facing up to change. Middle age and death are part of life's realities. Lammas magic can be magic of detachment. It is a time to let go of past grief and anger and move forward. This is a good time for divorce. It is also, paradoxically, a good time for marriage for people who intend being spiritual partners. This is not a good time for founding material enterprises, but can be a good time for spiritual ones.

Autumn Equinox

Autumn is the season of the apple harvest, the season of hops and grapes. Autumn Equinox is a celebration but also an ending of summer and a preparation for the cold to come.

Autumn magic is magic of the mind. It is time to start studying as the nights draw in and the outside world is less of a distraction. As the night-time world comes to dominate the year, it is also a time to develop our magical and psychic powers. The first half of the year is about the outer world. The second half is about the inner world and spiritual realm.

One way of celebrating Autumn is to float a candle down a river as a sign that the Sun is going away from us for a time. At this time, we celebrate the descent of the Goddess to the underworld.

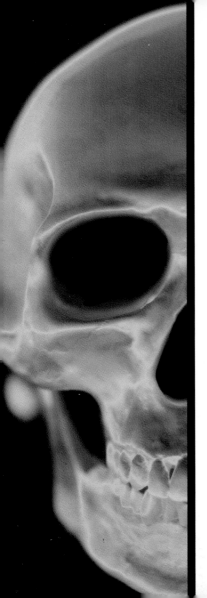

Samhain

Samhain is Irish for 'Summer's end'. Winter comes later to Ireland and to other western parts of Europe warmed by the Gulf stream.

Samhain is the festival of the dead. Modern society does everything it can to separate us from death, and many of us have little contact with the generations that preceded us, but a sense of who we are and where we have come from is important. We should honour the past and our forebears. Their hopes, fears, joys and sorrows are woven into the fabric of our psyches.

One way of celebrating Samhain is to build an altar to our ancestors: find old photographs, mementos, medals, and put them in a place of honour. Our spiritual ancestors are those whose dreams and visions have created the Wiccan spiritual life that we have today. For Samhain, why not do some research into our Pagan past?

Winter Solstice

Winter Solstice is the low point of the year in terms of daylight and energy. In our heated houses with enough food to eat all year, it is difficult for us to understand the perils of winter. In the past, there was always a danger that if winter was long, food might run out.

At Winter Solstice, the wheel of the year reaches its lowest point and shortest day, and then – the great miracle – the day grows just marginally longer. Winter Solstice, or Yule, was a time for feasting. It was a time to decorate the house with greenery and bright red-berried holly, to burn the biggest logs, to bake sweet honeyed cakes, to buy treats for the children. All these were ways to affirm hope in the dark time and to bring a little colour and joy into winter.

Exercise:
Communing with Nature

If we want to celebrate the seasonal cycle, how can we begin? The sabbats celebrate the changing face of Nature. To begin to understand them, we must get outside. As near as you can to the sabbat, go for a walk, ideally in the countryside, or if not in a city park. Look at what is going on in Nature around you. Are the trees budding, in blossom, in full leaf, fruiting, covered with dead leaves or bare? What are the birds doing, the animals, the flowers?

Time spent with nature can be healing. Life in cities is unnatural and stressful. When rats are overcrowded, they attack one another. When humans are overcrowded we get neighbourhood violence and road rage. Solitude, silence and greenness are strongly advocated in Wicca. To be alone with Nature; to have times of silence, solitude and peace; all this enables us to hear the inner voices of the Gods, to learn their will and to reflect on how we can live better and more wisely.

Exercise:
Creating a seasonal altar

An altar is a focal point for worship and for veneration of the Divine powers of the universe. An altar can be anywhere. You can make one simply by placing symbols of the four elements on a shelf, table or desk in your home or workplace, or in your garden.

1 Decide where to create your altar. Usually, Wiccan altars are in the north of a room, or in the centre with their backs to the north.
2 You can use a small table, a shelf or a chest for your altar. You may want to cover it with a piece of cloth appropriate to the season.
3 You will need something to represent each of the four elements: candles for Fire; incense, a feather or bell for Air; a bowl of water for Water; and a bowl of earth or a rock for Earth.
4 Now you have the beginnings of your altar, you need appropriate seasonal decorations. Go for a walk and try to find some seasonal flowers or greenery to bring home for your altar.

5 Once you have made your altar, take some time to meditate in front of it. Festivals begin at Sunset, so this is a good time to begin, but if this is not practical then you can begin your meditation at any time.

6 First light a candle and some incense if you have it. Think about the themes of the festival. How might they apply to your life? Ask the Gods to assist you with any problems that you may have at this time. Take a piece of paper, write down your problems and leave it hidden somewhere on or under the altar. When it is time to change your altar, read it to see if there have been any changes in your situation and then burn your requests in a candle flame. Maybe the Gods will have heard you, maybe not; but it is important to ask, to articulate our need.

7 Communing with Nature and making a seasonal altar are ways of beginning to celebrate the sabbats. Later you might want to create some sabbat rituals (*see page* 84).

Magic

Some people are more attracted to the Nature religion side of Wicca, others to its magic-making, others to a combination of these. But what is magic?

Magic is causing change by means not yet accepted by science. There are two types of magic – natural magic and high magic. We use high magic to transform ourselves into more evolved human beings. In Wicca, high magic involves initiatory rites and rites of worship which put us in touch with the Divine within and without. We will look at these later.

Natural magic

Natural magic seeks to cause changes on the material plane rather than inner changes. It uses the properties of certain external things, such as crystals and metals, herbs, planetary and lunar influences; harnessing their energies and flowing with their tides. Magic can also involve the agency of third parties – angels, spirits, elementals, but this is not so common in Wicca as it is in some forms of ritual magic. Wicca tends to rely mostly on the innate knowledge and abilities of the Witch – the powers of the human mind.

Divination

Wicca today works with and develops the powers of parapsychology. These are telepathy – knowing what someone else is thinking or feeling; clairvoyance – obtaining information about the future; psychometry – finding information about things by touching them; dowsing – using a pendulum or divining rod to locate things; and psychokinesis – causing physical change through the use of the mind. The latter is often called magic and the former skills are lumped together under the heading of divination.

Magic involves the active use and projection of our inner powers. Clairvoyance is about learning to be still, passive and receptive. Clairvoyants are those who by birth or training are more able than the rest of us to notice subtle signals. Part of Wiccan training is to become more aware of 'weak' signals. These signals are stronger when we are relaxed, meditating or dreaming. By learning to remember our dreams, we become more open to other messages from the unconscious in our waking life. These are the premonitions, dreams and hunches which people experience but often ignore.

Who can do magic?

In most traditional societies, Witchcraft was the prerogative of a trained professional – Shaman, Medicine Man, Witch Doctor, Cunning Man, Wise Woman, Witch. These professional practitioners often inherited their 'businesses' from a mother or father. In some societies, they were people who had undergone a special spiritual crisis. They were chosen by the Gods and set apart.

Traditional Witches often held the view that Witches are born, not made. In modern times, attitudes have changed. This is why old Craft teachers started to bring outsiders into their traditions; not to be 'professional Witches' but to learn to integrate the magical arts into their everyday lives.

People often come into Wicca saying, 'I'd like to be a Witch but I don't know if I'd be any good at magic.' Most Witches are better at some aspects of Wicca than others. However, we can all develop some magical skills.

It is not even essential to believe before you practise. What is important is not unshakeable belief, but open-mindedness.

How do we do magic?

Many objects used in magic have no inherent value of their own but can carry a 'charge' of our energy and serve as props to aid concentration. Traditional objects include cords, candles and wax images. These are useful props, but what are more important are the internal processes that go on within the Witch. Four important things are:

- visualization
- concentration
- trance
- etheric energy.

❑ Visualization

Magic works using visual images. If you have a vivid imagination, you will find visualization easy. If not you will need to practise. Try looking around your room. Close your eyes and visualize just one part of the room and the objects in it. Open your eyes and check how well you have done. Practise this technique whenever you can.

❑ Concentration

Magic requires concentration. This can be difficult, particularly if we find it difficult to 'switch off'. Do not worry too much about your mind wandering when you first start to practise magic. If you notice your mind has wandered off, simply pull it gently back.

☐ Trance

Trance involves moving into an altered state of consciousness and entering a timeless zone. This need not involve losing awareness of everyday reality, but the focus of attention is elsewhere. Things that can induce relaxation such as incense, candle light, firelight, chakra exercises, soft music, chanting, dance and drumming will help us enter a trance state. These are the psychotechnology of all spiritual and magical traditions.

☐ Etheric Energy

Witches have always believed that the body has certain energies that can be directed to achieve a particular end. As well as a physical body, we also have an etheric body. This is an energy field that surrounds and permeates the physical body. The etheric body has special energy centres that in Sanskrit are called chakras or wheels. These are points whereby the etheric body transmits and receives energy. There are seven major chakras in the body.

Exercise:

Opening the chakras

Opening our energy centres, the chakras, is helpful when we are about to do magic. It will ensure that we have energy to project and that our own energy store does not become depleted.

1 To open the chakras, first visualize a round circle of pulsating red light at the base of your spine. Now imagine that you are drawing a current of energy into the chakra so that it grows warm and begins to glow and pulsate with red energy and light. Visualize the base of spine chakra growing larger until it covers the whole of your lower spine.

2 Then, as the flow of energy comes into your body, allow it to coil round and round inside you like a snake. Allow the snake of energy to rise, still spiralling, until it reaches the level of your belly.

3 As it does so, visualize your sacral chakra in the centre of your belly beginning to glow with spinning orange light. Allow the orange circle to grow larger and larger, spinning with energy.

4 Continue to work your way up the body in this way, drawing energy in at the base of the spine, allowing it to spiral up the body and activate each chakra in turn.

5 At the level of the solar plexus is the solar plexus chakra that glows with a golden yellow light.

6 At the centre of the breast bone, there is a green fiery glow which is the heart chakra.

7 At the throat there is a pulsating blue centre, which is the throat chakra.

8 Past the throat, at the centre of the forehead, is the violet spot at the third eye.

9 As the violet glow of the third eye spins faster and faster, allow the current of energy to shoot up through the head and out of the crown chakra. Allow the energy to cascade down your body, bathing it in light, and flowing down to your feet in a white stream. Repeat this a few times and then relax.

Exercise:

Feeling etheric energy

Once you have opened your chakras, this is a simple exercise you can do to help you become more aware of your etheric energy.

Open your chakras. Imagine the solar plexus chakra activating the area around the middle of your body. Now allow energy from your solar plexus chakra to flow into your arms and into your hands. Visualize your hands beginning to glow with yellow light. If you find that channelling energy is draining, go back to the base of the spine and draw energy into yourself more frequently.

Now close your eyes and slowly bring the palms of your hands together until you can feel the energy from one hand pressing against the other. Open your eyes and see how far apart your hands were when you began to sense your energy. If you do this exercise frequently, you will find that your ability to project energy from hand to hand will grow stronger.

Exercise:
Closing the chakras

If we have opened the chakras, we must also close them. This can be done more quickly than opening them. One of the easiest ways is to imagine each chakra as a stained glass window of the appropriate colour.

1 Starting at the top, the crown chakra, draw a fountain of white light down the outside of your whole body. Let it flow over the third eye, closing the chakra completely as though a white shutter is being drawn over it.

2 Then draw more white light down from the crown past the third eye to the throat chakra, and then over the throat, shutting the chakra.

3 Draw more light from the crown down and over the heart chakra, over the solar plexus chakra, over the sacral and down to the base of the spine.

4 Do not attempt to close the base of spine chakra or crown chakras. These are left open to absorb energy.

What should we use magic for?

Magic is a force, a power, a wisdom, a knowledge. It is both more and less powerful than the ignorant suppose. In Wicca, magic is carried out according to strict ethics. Magic is not a crutch for the weak, nor an ego-boost for the inadequate. It is a skill that we must learn to use wisely and well.

Most people do not come to Wicca seeking magical training in order to make money and gain power. The usual problem is not people wanting to do negative magic, but people wanting to use their new-found powers to put the world to rights.

Some covens believe that you should not do magic for yourself. In most covens, however, people can work for themselves providing the group thinks it is appropriate.

There is a traditional Witchcraft saying, 'If it harms none, do what you will.' We must combine love with common sense, worldly wisdom and spiritual insight if magic is to do its work.

When is the best time?

There is a traditional saying in Witchcraft, 'Better it be when the Moon is full.' The Moon exacts a powerful pull on our world. It is the Earth's only natural satellite and it reflects the light and energy of the Sun. The Moon influences many of our physical rhythms.

For religions such as Wicca, which traditionally had most rituals outside at night, the Full Moon has practical benefits. It is much easier to see your way into and out of a wood when the Moon is Full. However, the Moon also affects our psychic abilities. This may be due to its physiological effect, or for more complex reasons; but making magic is much easier when the Moon is Full.

Planetary influences

Another influence on our magical timing is the planets. Experienced astrologers will calculate to the exact minute the right time to carry out a magical act so as to best harness particular planetary energies, but we can work with the planetary energies by knowing their attributes and doing our magic on the most appropriate day of the week

Day of the week	Planetary Ruler	Planetary Symbol	Oils	Colour	Appropriate Magic
Sunday	Sun	☉	Frankincense	Yellow, gold	Wealth, health
Monday	Moon	☽	Camphor	White, violet	Psychic matters, healing
Tuesday	Mars	♂	Ginger	Red	Strength
Wednesday	Mercury	♄	Lavender	Yellow, orange	Wisdom, teaching the mind
Thursday	Jupiter	☿	Cedar	Blue	Good fortune, prosperity, good humour
Friday	Venus	♃	Almond	Green	Love
Saturday	Saturn	♀	Storax	Brown	stability, earthing, saving money

Exercise:
Candle magic

Candle magic is a simple and traditional magical technique. It is good for drawing positive energy into our lives. Candle magic can be useful if people ask us to do magic for them. A candle can be consecrated and anointed and the other person can burn it for him - or herself.

1 First decide on your intent. Next, create a visual image that represents you achieving your intent.

2 Select an appropriate colour candle and decide an appropriate day on which to begin the magic. Have a look back at the table opposite.

3 Next, prepare an altar with symbols of the four elements on it. You will need candles for light as well as a new candle for your magic. You will also need some oil and a spare candlestick. You can buy an appropriate aromatherapy or magical oil or use pure olive oil.

4 Draw the curtains to block out any light and light the altar candles. Incense is helpful, and playing soft music will help you relax.

5 Open your chakras.

6 Visualize your intent and at the same time channel energy into your hands. Take your candle and hold it for a few moments, focusing on your intent.

7 Now take the oil and put a small amount on your fingers. Energize your base of spine chakra and draw energy into your hands once more. Anoint the candle, starting in the middle and smoothing the oil towards each end. While you anoint the candle, focus on your intent and create a visual image of your wish coming to pass.

8 Now use a candle that is already burning to light your new candle. Place it in its candlestick. Ask the Goddess and God to bless your magical intent.

9 The candle can now be left to burn. Usually candles are not burned in one session but over a period of either a week, starting and ending on the same day, or a lunar month. If you are dealing with a complex situation, then the magic will take longer.

10 The most difficult part of candle magic is discipline. People are always keen to do magic, but few people have the concentration to keep up such a simple thing as lighting a candle every evening over a period of eight days. If we cannot do this, then we do not have sufficient will to bring about the change we seek.

11 In candle magic, we do not have to focus on the candle all the time it is burning. However, we must think about our intent each time we light the candle and when we extinguish it.

12 As you extinguish the candle, here are some things you can say:

As I extinguish this flame on the Earthly plane,
may it burn more brightly in the realm of spirit
and bring my intent to birth.
Strong as the wind is my will,
strong as fire is my desire,
strong as the sea, my spell shall be,
strong as the Earth which gives it birth.
so mote it be!

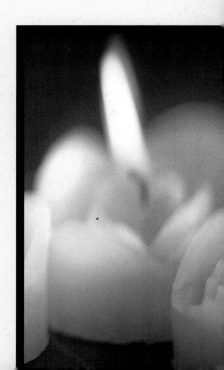

The Gods

In Wicca, experience is emphasized over belief, doctrine and dogma. Our Pagan ancestors performed rites but professed no creed or doctrine. The Goddess is the principle around which we base our lives. We do not believe in her; she just is. Wicca is the Old Religion. We worship the earliest forms of deity that the human mind and heart conceived – the Great Mother Goddess and her consort the Horned God. They are ways for us to approach the ineffable mystery – the one great spirit that gives life to the universe. In Wicca, this is often called the life force, the Divine, the essence, the power that moves the Universe. It is outside us, beyond us; yet within our innermost selves. We see its work in the changing face of Nature, the seasonal cycle that echoes the pattern of the universe – creation, maturation, decay, death and rebirth.

In reality our Gods do not have gender. We may choose to portray and understand them as Goddess and God, female and male, however, these are but ways for the human mind to grapple with and come to an intuitive understanding of the Divine force which is beyond human form.

To develop further in Wicca, we must be able to build a personal relationship with the Gods. We venerate with each season's change the aspect of the God and Goddess most appropriate to that time.

The Great Mother Goddess

Our earliest ancestors made crude Goddess figures. These Goddesses were big women. They had rounded bellies. Their sexual and fertility organs – breasts and vulva – were emphasized; for fertility was essential to the life of the people.

  In Wicca, the Goddess is still worshipped in her ancient names – as Aradia, Cerridwen, Isis, Astarte, Dione, Melusine, Aphrodite, Dana and Arianrhod. Traditionally, the Wiccan Goddess is worshipped in triple form – as the Virgin who has not known motherhood, as the Mother, and as the Wise Woman, who is post-motherhood, she who acts as midwife to the Mother and as layer out at death. For women today, the triple Goddess may no longer be appropriate. Another way of thinking about the Goddess in Wicca is not as a trinity but as that most Wiccan of symbols – the pentagram.

Dark Moon

Spirit/Ether
Great Grandmother/Wise Woman

New Moon

Air
Maiden

Full Moon

Water
Mother

The Goddess

Waning Moon

Earth
Grandmother

Waxing Moon

Fire
Lover-Queen

A woman's life can be seen as a journey around the pentagram

The Five-Fold Goddess

Goddess Phase	Moon Phase	Goddess	Element
Maiden	New	Persephone	Air
Lover	Waxing	Aphrodite, Bride, Freya, Kali, Nephthys	Fire
Mother	Full	Hera, Iris	Water
Grandmother	Waning	Demeter, Frigga	Earth
Wise one, great grandmother	Dark	Hecate, Cerridwen	Ether/Spirit

Season	Quality	Magical Command	Magical Weapon
Imbolc	Joy, creation, the song, the head	To know (to expand the mind)	Knife
Spring Equinox, Beltane	Passion, union, vagina	To will (to assert and express ourselves)	Wand
Midsummer, Yule	Love, sustenance, womb	To dare (to brave physical rigours and to overcome fear)	Cup
Lammas, Autumn Equinox	Sorrow, separation, letting go	To keep silent (in order to digest and learn)	Shield
Samhain	Wisdom, death, rest, transformation, rebirth, initiation	To teach, to reveal	Cauldron, crystal ball

The God

The God in Wicca is co-equal with the Goddess and an essential part of the Wiccan world view. Deep within the deepest caves, we find paintings of the God of hunt and forest, the Horned God. To our ancestors horns were a symbol of power and strength and therefore of divinity. The Horned God appears in many different cultures throughout the world. In India, he is Parvati, Lord of the Animals; he is Pan of the Greeks and Cernunnos of the Celts, who in England is known as Herne. The different aspects of God in Wicca can be most easily understood in terms of the seasonal cycle and of the elements. The God is born as the Sun Child in the depths of winter and moves through the phases of life to enter the darkness, the Centre. From darkness he emerges into light to become the Sun Child once more. This is his spiral dance.

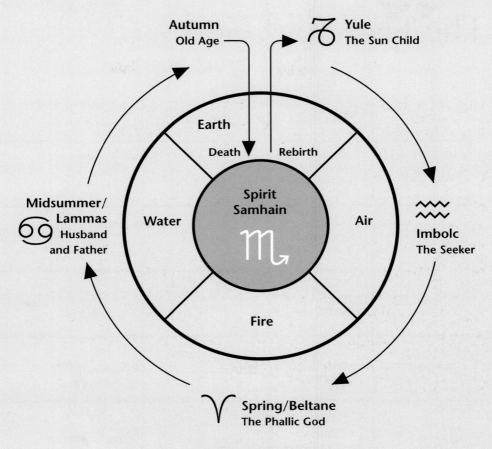

The God's Sabbat Journey

The Five-Fold God

Season	God Phase	Element	Quality
Yule, Imbolc	Child, young God	Air	Joy, creation, the song, the head
Spring Equinox, Beltane	Lover, Green Man, Phallic Lord	Fire	Passion, union, phallus
Midsummer, Yule	Husband, father, King	Water	Love, sustenance
Lammas, Autumn Equinox	Old God, sacrifice	Earth	Sorrow, separation, letting go
Samhain	Dark lord, initiator, Lord of Death	Ether/Spirit	Wisdom, death, rest, transformation, rebirth, initiation

Magical Command	Moon Phase	Magical Weapon
To know **(to expand** **the mind)**	**New**	Sword of Nuada
To will **(to assert and** **express ourselves)**	Waxing	Staff, rod, Spear of Lugh
To dare **(to brave physical** **rigours and to** **overcome fear)**	Full	Cup
To keep silent **(in order to digest** **and learn)**	Waning	Shield
To teach, **to reveal**	Dark	Cauldron, crystal ball

Exercise:
Pathworking

These two exercises are inner journeys to contact the Goddess and God. Begin by opening your chakras, and at the end record your experiences. Then close your chakras and earth yourself by eating and drinking. Do not do both excercises on the same day.

Goddess exercise

1 Visualize yourself standing in front of a black curtain on which is a silver Moon.

2 Now imagine the curtain becoming a transparent black veil through which you can see a landscape with a path leading through it.

3 Ask the permission of the Goddess to enter her kingdom and ask her to show you some of her secrets and symbols. Part the veil, step through it and begin to follow the path. When you feel you have reached the right place, stop and wait for the Goddess. If she appears she may have a message for you.

4 When you are ready to leave, bid the Goddess farewell. Return to the veil and step back through it.

God exercise

1 Visualize yourself standing at the top of a hill as a Full Moon rises.

2 You see a circle of standing stones ahead of you. There are people there. As you draw near, a space is made for you inside the circle.

3 Then, a figure appears and steps into the centre of the circle. He is very tall and on his head you see the antlers of a stag. There is a fire burning near the centre of the circle and its flames light up his face.

4 Then you hear his voice speaking softly. He is calling you to come to him.

5 You cross the circle and the God reaches out his hand. You sit down beside him by the fire.

6 You sit together, gazing into the flames. Allow him to tell you all that he feels you need to know.

7 The sky grows lighter. Dawn is approaching. You bid him farewell and then leave the stone circle as the first rays of morning Sun are beginning to dry the dew.

Ritual

Now that you know more about the Gods and about the seasonal cycle of Wicca, you can begin to think about creating rites of worship.

What will I need?

☐ Clothes

To create ritual, we need to separate ourselves off from the physical world. There are certain conventions that can help. One is that we wear no watch. Another is that we dress differently. We can wear a special robe, we can be skyclad, or naked, or we may simply remove our shoes. When we begin our ritual practice it is enough to remove our shoes and to wash ourselves. If you decide that you enjoy ritual, you may wish to buy or make a robe. A black outdoor robe and a white indoor one to which different colour cords can be added are versatile. Silk or cotton is fine for indoor working. Outside, wool or velvet are good,

warm materials. Natural materials are preferred to artificial ones. Not everyone feels comfortable with the idea of robes. An alternative is to keep some simple clothing that you use for ritual purposes.
Tai chi clothes or similar are excellent.

☐ Cords

When working robed or skyclad, Witches usually wear a cord around the waist. This symbolizes that they are bound to the Gods and is a reminder of their dedication to the Craft. The length is nine feet or three metres. In many traditions, certain colour cords indicate a certain level of initiation. You do not want to imply that you are claiming status you do not have. Neutral colours that are not used in this way are brown (for Earth) and white (to symbolize purity of intent).

☐ Jewellery

Many Witches wear the five-pointed star or the Egyptian looped cross, the ankh. Another practice of female Witches is to wear an amber necklace. The necklace's circular shape is reminiscent of all circles and cycles, including those of conception, birth, death and rebirth.

☐ Water and Salt

Witches often keep spring water for rites. Salt is added to the water to consecrate and purify it. At the end of the rite, any unused water is poured into the ground at a spot where the salt will not damage growing plants. Do not pour it down the kitchen sink! Once you have made something sacred, you must treat it with respect.

☐ Incense

You can use joss sticks or incense sticks for your incense, but loose incense, burned on charcoal blocks, smells much better. In Wiccan ritual, censing takes place early in the rite and is part of the cleansing process that clears the way for raising magical energies.

☐ Candles

Indoors we use candles to light our sacred space. One or two candles are usually placed on the altar. Four candles are placed at the edge of the sacred space – one in each of the four quarters – blue in the East (Air); red in the South (Fire); bluey-green in the West (Water) and brown in the North (Earth).

☐ Wand

An ancient magical tool that we can use to channel our magical energy is a wand. Wands can be used to cast a circle and invoke the quarters.

A consecrated knife called an athame can also be used. An advantage of a wand is that it is much easier to obtain than an athame. There is an exercise on page 78 to help you find a wand.

☐ Cup and Plate

You will need a chalice or goblet and an ornamental plate or a small basket for the blessing of cakes, or bread and wine. Bread or cakes that you have made yourself are ideal; so too is home-made wine. Mead or ale can also be used. If you prefer not to drink alcohol, use grape or apple juice.

Exercise:
Finding a wand

You have already learned to channel energy into your hands. This is essential for magical practice. The next step is to learn how to channel your energy into a wand.

To choose a type of wood, look up the symbolism of different trees in a book such as Robert Graves' *The White Goddess* or Jacqueline Memory Paterson's *Tree Wisdom*, or just see which tree draws you.

First find your tree. Avoid cutting wood if you can. If there is newly-fallen wood, take it. If you need to cut some, spend some time in meditation, then approach the tree with respect. Explain what you want the wood for and ask for the tree's permission. Then cut it as cleanly as possible. Take only what you need.

Some people carve intricate patterns, shapes and symbols on their Wands. Others prefer to adapt only slightly the natural beauty of the wood. Do whatever feels most appropriate. Generally however, some working of the wood is a good idea as this starts to make it truly yours.

Exercise:
Consecrating your wand

Now you have your wand, you must devise a ritual to consecrate it. Write some words that offer the wand to the Gods as a tool for the channelling of their energy and power. Ask them to help you use your wand wisely and well.

On a day when the Moon is between New and Full, set up an altar. Open your chakras and channel energy into your hands. Consecrate your wand with the elements by passing it through incense smoke and through a candle flame, sprinkling it with water and pressing it against Earth. As you pass the wand through each element, ask the element to bless your wand and say your words of dedication.

Hold your wand and point it above the altar. Channel energy into your hands and down the wand. Visualize the tip of the wand glowing with your energy and power. Now draw the invoking pentagram of Fire (see page 80) in the air above the altar with your new wand. Visualize this pentagram for as long as you can and then banish it by drawing the banishing pentagram (reversing the invoking pentagram), withdrawing the lines of energy back into your wand.

Now close down your chakras and extinguish your altar lights and incense. Wrap your wand in a piece of silk, cotton or wool and put it away. Make notes on this, your first simple ritual. What did you feel, see? How do you feel now the ritual is done?

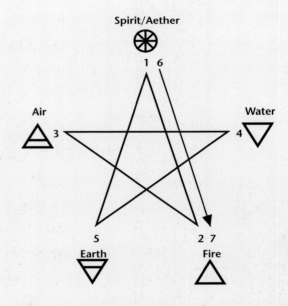

Invoking pentagram of fire

Sabbat rites

Witches celebrate the eight seasonal festivals of Wicca and also the 13 Full Moons. They are a time to worship the Gods and to do magical work. A good way to start to become familiar with ritual is to create eight seasonal rites over the course of the year. In this way, you will harmonize your life with the rhythms of Nature and of the cosmos.

In Wicca we are expected to know ritual and spells by heart. At first this seems daunting. Just learn a bit each time. After a while you will be able to learn complex rites without difficulty.

Exercise:
Creating invocations

To create a ritual, we need to call upon, or invoke, the Goddess and God. An invocation is an invitation for the power of the Goddess or God to make itself manifest in the circle and in our lives. You can find many invocations in books, but it is better to try writing your own. How might you create an invocation for a sabbat?

Let us think about Lammas. If we go out into the countryside, what do we see? There might be fields of ripened wheat swaying in the breeze. Above may be a clear blue sky and occasional cloud. The earth will be warm to the touch after months of Sun. Maybe a sudden summer storm might appear – black clouds and hail which threaten to flatten the wheat.

How might we think of the God at this time? As the tall straight stalks of wheat reaching up to the Sun? How might we think of the Goddess? As the warm earth from whose womb the corn springs forth? As the women with sickles who in ancient times would come and reap the wheat and separate grain from chaff?

From these images we can create an invocation.

Hail Lord of the Golden Wheat
tall and proud in the Summer Sun;
Hail voice of the wind, calling his destiny,
sacrifice yourself before the will of the people.
Hail unto Thee, Great Mother of All,
Thy symbol the sickle, the taker of life.
From Thy womb, Thou bringest forth life in abundance,
wheat and flower, food and beauty,
from the deep rich earth that shall be the tomb of all.
We invoke Thee.

Now try it for yourself – take the images of the next sabbat to come and play with them in your mind. Make them your own living reality and, from the centre of your heart, create words that express your feelings.

Exercise:
Creating a sabbat ritual

First, think of an appropriate theme for your sabbat. Wherever you live you must celebrate the seasonal festivals appropriately. If you live in the southern hemisphere transpose all the northern hemisphere festival dates by six months. If you live in a climate that is different from temperate Europe, you may need to adapt the seasonal festivals.

1. Preparing for the Rite

You must prepare yourself and the place in which you are to do your rite. Clean and tidy your space. Set out your altar and magical equipment. Decorate the altar in a way appropriate to the season. Prepare yourself: bathe or shower, put on your robe. Switch off the phone.

2. Opening the Rite

Centre yourself by opening the chakras or, if your ritual is outside, just sitting quietly and listening to the sounds of Nature. Now open the rite. Say something to the Gods to state your purpose. Take the images that the festival calls to your mind and create a prayer.

3. Creating the Circle

Now cast your circle. First consecrate water. Take your wand and channel power down it from your solar plexus chakra. Place the point of the wand in the water and say some words of blessing. Now bless the salt in the same way. Sprinkle some salt in the water. Sprinkle the water on the ground around the edge of the circle. Start at the North and walk deosil, or clockwise, around the circle until you come back to the starting point. Next, take incense and carry it around the perimeter of your sacred space; again from North to North.

4. Sealing the Sacred Space

Now you must create a boundary between the space and the outside world. Take your wand and go to the North of your circle. Channel energy down your hands and along your wand. Visualize a glowing light at the tip of the wand. Hold your wand at waist height, pointing it outwards. Now walk deosil around your circle drawing a line of light and energy in the air. Some words for casting the circle are: 'I draw with wand the circle round, love be raised and power be bound. By the Might of the Moon and the Horns of Herne, be this sacred circle formed. So mote it be.'

5. Calling on the Quarters

Now you must call upon the elemental energies at the four quarters to guard your rite. Before calling upon the quarters, you need to visualize a scene appropriate to the element.

Air: go to the East of the circle. Stand facing outwards. Visualize yourself in a high place, the wind blowing on your face. See, feel and hear the presence of the element, and then, when you are ready, say: 'Ye Mighty Ones of the East, Powers of Air, I summon, stir and call ye up to guard my circle and witness my rite.' Once you have felt the presence of the elemental forces, say: 'Hail and Welcome!'

Fire: now walk deosil around the circle to the South. Stand facing outwards. Visualize a blazing Sun which grows larger and larger until it fills your vision. You feel its heat and flames but they do not burn. Summon the element as before.

Water: now walk deosil around the circle to the West. Stand facing outwards. Visualize a blue-green sea, the waves crashing against the shore. Now invoke the West and welcome the Powers of Water as before.

Earth: now walk deosil around the circle to the North. Stand facing outwards. Visualize a standing stone. Feel the rough, lichen covered stone. Smell the musty, damp, rich smell of Earth. Now invoke the North and the Powers of Earth.

6. Raising Power

In coven Witchcraft, the coven will frequently dance and chant at this point to raise energy for magical work. If you are working on your own, you can chant and dance in a deosil circle around your altar if it is in the centre. If you do not want to dance, you can chant quietly, perhaps watching a candle flame. If you have a drum, you could drum.

7. Worshipping the Gods

Before doing any magical work, we call upon the Goddess and God to bless our endeavours and to ensure that they accord with the Divine will. You can find invocations from books or write your own. First, visualize an image of the Goddess you have developed from your meditations. Imagine her presence, first as a misty form and then becoming more concrete. When you can feel her energy, say your invocation. Now do the same for the God.

8. Spells and Magical Work

Once we have called upon the Gods to bless our endeavours, we perform any magical work that needs to be done. Not all rituals are for magic. We may create a rite for worship and celebration only.

9. Celebration

Once we have worshipped our Gods and performed our magic, it is good to celebrate by blessing cakes and wine. These represent the food and sustenance that the Gods have provided for us. Offer first the cakes and then the wine to the Goddess and God, asking their blessing as you eat of their bounty. In a group, the offering is passed around the circle of participants and a ceremonial greeting is exchanged: 'Blessèd Be'. The last of the cakes and wine is scattered and poured out on the Earth as a libation. In this way, we return of little of what we have taken.

10. Closing the Rite

Firstly, we say a prayer of thanksgiving to the Gods for their blessing and assistance. Then we bid farewell to the quarters. The elements are powerful forces. It is important that you do not have excess energy wandering around. Go to each of the quarters as before, starting in the East and finishing in the North. Face outwards and address the quarters.

Ye Mighty Ones of the East (South, West, North),
Powers of Air (Fire, Water, Earth),
I thank you for attending my rite
and ere you depart to your fair and lovely realms,
I bid you: hail and farewell!

11. Closing Down the Chakras

A final stage is to close down our chakras. Within the circle, we want to be as open as possible to the energies we have raised. Outside the circle we want to have control over what impinges on our psychic space.

'The rite is ended!'

Today, many have answered the call of the Goddess and of the Lord of the Woods to build a new spiritual vision for the Age to come. So this book is theirs, although I cannot hope to fully tell their story; but we who share it will in the coming years dance it, sing it and little by little, word by word, come nearer to the truth.

Remember: Wicca is a way of being, of life, of love, of joy, of laughter, of accepting that life can be painful and tough, while doing what we can to make it a better place for others and for ourselves.

Be blessed, be happy, be wise,
laugh and love!
This is the way of Goddess and God.
Blessèd Be!